The *Kerygma*

A Model For Proclaiming the Christian Gospel

Peter Briggs

The Two Ways cover picture was created by Louis Pecastaing of Albuquerque, NM. Used by permission.

Unless otherwise noted, all Scripture quotations are taken from *The Holy Bible, New King James Version*, Copyright © 1979, 1980, 1982 by Thomas Nelson, Inc. Used by permission. All rights reserved.

ISBN-10: 1-947642-08-1
ISBN-13: 978-1-947642-08-9

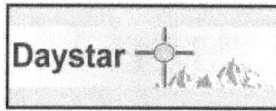

Published by: Distributed in Africa by:
Daystar Institute / NM, Inc.   Daystar Institute / Africa
P.O. Box 50567   P.O. Box 3989 00200
Albuquerque, New Mexico   Nairobi, Kenya
87181-0567 USA
www.DaystarInstituteNM.us   www.DaystarInstituteAfrica.org

TABLE OF CONTENTS

LIST OF FIGURES

Foreword

The Kerygma: A Model For Proclaiming the Christian Gospel has been extracted from Part 4 of the theological reader for the study entitled *Walking in the Way of Christ and the Apostles* (WitW). It is published as a booklet for ease of use and maximum accessibility.

For some time I have been contemplating the preparation of a booklet on the proclamation of the Christian gospel that reflects the WitW study. I represent WitW as a study in practical Christian theology, uncompromising discipleship, and building a biblical worldview. The four-part theological reader for the WitW study consists of seventeen chapters, each of which corresponds to a study guide booklet. The entire WitW study is laid out on the inside back cover of this booklet.

Your fellow servant,

Peter Briggs

The Kerygma: A Model For Proclaiming the Christian Gospel

Introduction

Scripture presents the Christian gospel in two interconnected and mutually complementary aspects: the **gospel of the kingdom of God**, and the **gospel of God**. These two aspects are summarized in Figure 1.

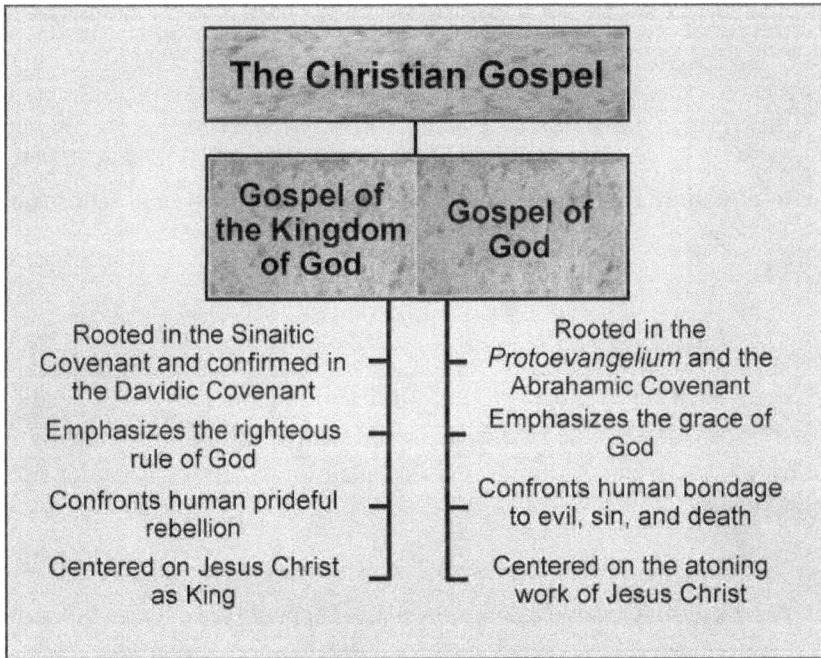

Figure 1. The Two-Part Christian Gospel

The gospel of the kingdom of God is emphasized in the Synoptic Gospels and the Book of Acts, and it appeals most strongly to Jewish mind. The gospel of God is emphasized in the Pauline epistles, and it appeals most strongly to the Gentile mind. A balanced gospel proclamation must reflect both aspects of the Christian gospel. In particular, we must not only receive and believe the gospel in accordance with John 1:12-13, but we must also obey it by becoming devoted followers of Jesus Christ who are submitted to His kingly rule.

The Greek word *kerygma* is a technical term in the Greek New Testament that designates the Christian gospel proclaimed by the apostles as recorded in the Book of Acts. The verb form of this word is *kerusso*, which signifies a formal proclamation, such as would be made by an ambassador on behalf of the head of state of the nation which he represents.   This word is entirely appropriate to represent the proclamation of the Christian gospel on the basis of the Apostle Paul's assertion in 2 Corinthians 5:20-21. The Lord Jesus Christ, seated on His heavenly throne, has commissioned and charged us, His followers, to serve as His ambassadors as we proclaim the good news of deliverance from bondage to evil, sin, and death which has been brought about by His redemptive work on Calvary's Cross.

With *kerygma* designating the manner in which the apostles proclaimed the Christian gospel as recorded in the Book of Acts, it behooves us to carefully study examples of apostolic gospel proclamation and pattern our proclamation after theirs.

The Two Ways

To provide a suitable background for discussing the *kerygma*, I need to first briefly discuss the **two ways** as revealed in Scripture. **The way** is a technical term in Scripture that designates a pattern of behavior or a lifestyle.

> *The true character of a person is placed in evidence by his way. In other words, a person's way is the visible manifestation of what is in his heart.*

The 1ˢᵗ Psalm is a cogent representation of the two ways: the way of the **righteous** that leads to eternal life, and the way of the **wicked** that leads to ruin and eternal death. In Matthew 7:13-14, Jesus Christ speaks of a narrow gate that opens into a narrow and difficult way, and a wide gate that opens into a broad, inviting, and easy way. The narrow and difficult way leads to eternal life, and the broad, inviting, and easy way leads to ruin and eternal death. These two ways are illustrated in Figure 2.

Figure 2. The Two Ways

Directing your attention to Figure 2, notice that the wide gate is open, but the narrow gate is closed. All of us, without exception, begin our pilgrimage through this present life on the broad, inviting, and easy way that leads to ruin and eternal death. It is only by a deliberate choice and an intentional act that we make the transition to the narrow and difficult way that leads to eternal life. The key that unlocks the narrow gate is **faith**.

The kind of faith of which I am speaking is not merely a mental assent to the facts of the Christian gospel, but rather a wholehearted embrace and trust in a Person – namely, Jesus Christ, the Son of God.

> *The kind of faith that brings salvation necessarily produces a heart transformation and a way that conforms to the way of Christ. A person with this kind of faith surrenders all that he is and has to Christ and follows Him as His obedient disciple.*

The Peril of Nominalism

With the two ways now clearly in view, I need to address the peril of **nominalism**. Tragically, the proclamation of the Christian gospel in the West has been seriously compromised since the early part of the 19th century. As a result, many people who attend church services and behave religiously are Christians in name only – CINO. They were taught that a person need only give a mental assent to the facts of the gospel, and then offer a one-time prayer to receive Christ as Savior. For such a person, a surrendered and obedient lifestyle is entirely optional.

The error in this representation of Christian discipleship is clearly placed in evidence by the vision of the Apostle John as recorded in the 21st chapter of Revelation.

> **Revelation 21:7-8.** He who overcomes shall inherit all things, and I will be his God and he shall be My son. But the cowardly, unbelieving, abominable, murderers, sexually immoral, sorcerers, idolaters, and all liars shall have their part in the lake which burns with fire and brimstone, which is the second death.

Repeatedly in the writings of the Apostles, the Christian life is likened to a marathon race. In order to qualify for the prize, **one must finish the race**. This entails overcoming one's own physical and emotional limitations as well as the other contestants in the race. The marathon race analogy provides a glimpse into the meaning of the passage quoted above.

> *Raising one's hand in an evangelistic service, going forward at an invitation, and offering a one-time prayer is, at best, only the start of the Christian pilgrimage. Entrance into Christ's eternal kingdom requires that we finish the course marked out for us.*

From the passage in the 21ˢᵗ chapter of Revelation quoted above, the fact is evident that there are but two ultimate destinations for each of us. The desirable destination is Christ's eternal kingdom, a glimpse of which is afforded by the vision of the Apostle John in the closing chapters of the Book of Revelation. The other destination is represented as a "lake that burns with fire and brimstone." It is a place of eternal torment. The Apostle Paul describes this second destination as follows in the 1ˢᵗ chapter of 2 Thessalonians:

> **2 Thessalonians 1:7-10.** ... And to give you who are troubled rest with us when the Lord Jesus is revealed from heaven with His mighty angels, in flaming fire taking vengeance on those who do not know God, and on those who do not obey the gospel of our Lord Jesus Christ. These shall be punished with everlasting destruction from the presence of the Lord and from the glory of His power, when He comes, in that Day, to be glorified in His saints and to be admired among all those who believe, because our testimony among you was believed.

The broad, inviting, and easy way leads to a destination that must be avoided at all costs. The narrow and difficult way leads to a destination that must be pursued at all costs.

A Canonical Outline of One Component of the Kerygma

In 1 Corinthians 15:1-8, especially the 3ʳᵈ through the 8ᵗʰ verses, we find a canonical outline of one component of the *kerygma*; to wit, a succinct, mnemonically appealing sequence of points which emphasizes the factuality of Christ's resurrection, this emphasis being consistent with the overall thrust of the 15ᵗʰ chapter. The pattern of 1 Corinthians 15:3-8 suggests that Paul was quoting from an ancient 1ˢᵗ century confession. In fact, biblical scholars convincingly argue that Paul had been taught this ancient confession by Peter and James during his first visit to Jerusalem after his conversion, as recorded in Acts 9:26-30. Note the essential points in Paul's argument as follows:

> ### 1 Corinthians 15:3-6:
> *For I delivered to you first of all that which I also received:*
> *that Christ died for our sins according to the Scriptures,*
> *and that He was buried,*
> *and that He rose again the third day according to the Scriptures,*
> *and that He was seen by Cephas,*
> *then by the twelve.*
> *After that He was seen by over five hundred brethren at once,*
> *of whom the greater part remain to the present...*

Paul's Theological Agenda in the 15th Chapter of 1 Corinthians

Paul's theological agenda in the 15th chapter of 1 Corinthians is twofold: first, to establish the fact of Jesus' resurrection; and, second, to place in evidence the implications of His resurrection for the life and ministry of the disciple. This theological agenda was motivated by the heresy which was troubling the Corinthian church as summarized in the 12th verse; namely, that there was no such thing as the resurrection from the dead. In support of his theological agenda, Paul distills the gospel down to a confession that testifies to the factuality of Jesus' resurrection. The following paragraphs briefly summarize each of the points in his argument.

Christ Died. The death of Jesus Christ is an actual historical event that took place in approximately 31 AD in accordance with the prophecies of the Hebrew Scriptures. In fact, the historical narrative of the Hebrew Scriptures sets forth the reason or motivation for the sacrificial death of Christ by placing in evidence the problem of evil, sin, and death. This problem invaded the cosmos at the dawn of human history, and it has universally impacted the human race. Apart from the narrative of the Hebrew Scriptures, Jesus' death could only be regarded as absurd and pointless.

He Was Buried. Jesus' sacrificial death was actual. He did not simply faint on the Cross and later recover. According to John 19:32-35, Pilate explicitly commissioned soldiers to verify the death of the three crucified individuals, and one of them thrust a spear into Jesus' side to ensure that He was actually dead. Accordingly, Jesus Christ really died in the presence of a multitude of witnesses, His body was tenderly prepared for burial by Joseph of Arimathea and Nicodemus, and He was sealed in a rock-cut tomb for three days and three nights.

He Was Raised. While details of the four gospel accounts seem to differ in regard to the fine-grained detail of exactly what took place on the morning that Christians celebrate as Easter Sunday, with regard to the empty tomb they all agree. In fact, according to Matthew 28:11-15, the Jewish leaders bribed the Roman soldiers to spread abroad the incredible story that **His disciples had stolen Jesus' body while they were asleep**. Imagine a soldier publishing such a report! By it he would have declared himself guilty of dereliction of duty, for which he would have been liable to execution.

> *The point of Matthew's account is clear: even Jesus' enemies confirmed that the tomb where He had been sealed, and which had been placed under guard by Roman soldiers, was now empty.*

The lexical form of the Greek verb that is translated **raised** in 1 Corinthian 15:4 is *egeiro*, which means to rise from a supine to an upright, standing position. Thus, Paul's representation precludes a non-physical, or spiritual resurrection.

Critical scholars assert that the resurrection was a fabrication of the early church in order to deify Jesus. Arguing against this theory, Paul's first epistle to the church at Corinth was written ca. 56 AD. Moreover, the ancient confession that Paul quotes in our focal passage was already embraced by the Christian community in Jerusalem shortly after the event in question; and it was probably conveyed by Peter and James to Paul during his first visit to Jerusalem after his conversion, as recorded in the 9th chapter of Acts. In fact, there is no reasonable explanation for the documentary evidence recorded by Luke in the Book of Acts other than this: the resurrection of Jesus Christ is historical fact, of which more than 500 people were eye witnesses; and most of them were still alive at the time 1 Corinthians was written. On account of their ringing testimony concerning the fact of Jesus' resurrection, all the apostles were executed except John, and he was exiled to the Isle of Patmos. No one would lay down his life for a testimony that he knew to be fabricated and false!

According to the Scriptures. According to Paul, the resurrection of Jesus Christ was in accordance with the prophecies of the Hebrew Scriptures – in particular, Psalm 16:10-11 and Isaiah 53:10-11.

He Appeared. Paul concludes this testimony concerning the factuality of Christ's resurrection by enumerating His post-resurrection appearances. In order to verify the historical factuality of the event, the members of his audience in Corinth could have interviewed literally hundreds of individuals who had actually seen the risen Christ. According to Paul in Romans 1:4, the resurrection demonstrates that Christ is the One He claimed to be; namely, "the Son of God with power..." Moreover, according to Romans 4:25, the fact of the resurrection confirms that Jesus' sacrificial death was adequate to procure for us justification and the gift of eternal life.

Summary of the Essential Components of the Kerygma

We need to include a number of other key points in our outline of the essential components of the *kerygma*. I propose that any proclamation of the gospel should reflect the following ten essential components:

1. In the beginning, God designed and created man to be a citizen in His perfect kingdom, submitting to His righteous rule, enjoying fellowship with Him, beholding His glory, and serving Him in worshipful obedience.

2. However, mankind very quickly fell prey to prideful rebellion in that we disobeyed the single prohibition that God laid upon us, as recorded in the 3rd chapter of Genesis.

3. As a result, prideful rebellion against the righteous rule of God has become a governing principle in our hearts, causing us to live as if He does not exist and to engage in attitudes, thoughts, words, and actions which contradict His righteous commandments. In other words, our way is the way of the wicked that leads to ruin and eternal death.

4.   The Bible defines **sin** as the falling short of the righteous commandments of God. Our sin is a capital offense against God, for which the penalty is death, as recorded in Genesis 2:17 in relation to the first prohibition that God laid upon mankind. Because of our prideful rebellion, and the sinful attitudes, thoughts, words, and behaviors engendered by it, it is impossible for us to submit to God's righteous rule, enjoy fellowship with Him, behold His glory, and serve Him in worshipful obedience – that is, to live in accordance with the purpose for which He designed and created us in the beginning.

5.   However, on account of His great love for us, and to showcase His glorious grace, God has provided a way for us to be rescued and delivered from bondage to evil, sin, and death and restored to a state in which we can fulfill the purpose for which He designed and created us.

6.   However, on account of His absolute justice, He cannot overlook the capital offense of which we are guilty. And so He sent His Son to become a Man in the person of Jesus of Nazareth, to walk in our sandals, to experience life as we know it, and to walk in the way of God in perfect obedience to His commandments. Accordingly, throughout His life and ministry, Jesus models perfectly the fulfillment of the glorious purpose for which God created mankind.

7.   Moreover, by means of His sacrificial death on Calvary's Cross, Jesus took upon Himself our sin, making it His personal responsibility. He experienced the equivalent of eternal hell in our place, paying back to God the Father the infinite apology and satisfaction each of us owe to Him on account of our sin.

8.   The fact of Jesus' resurrection authenticates that He is the Son of God with power in accordance with Romans 1:4; that His sacrificial death is sufficient to atone for our sin and procure for us the gifts of righteousness before God and eternal life in accordance with Romans 4:25; and that He is able to save to the uttermost all who come unto God by Him in accordance with Hebrews 7:25.

9.   By heartily repenting of our prideful rebellion against the righteous rule of God and embracing and appropriating Jesus' death in our place, God the Father responds by pardoning our sin, declaring us to be righteous in His sight, embracing us as adopted children and members of His family, and conferring upon us the gift of eternal life.

10.   This glorious transaction projects us onto a path of becoming progressively submitted to the righteous rule of God – that is, the narrow way that leads to eternal life. Moreover, we have the certain hope of becoming citizens of His eternal kingdom and being able to perfectly fulfill the purpose for which He created us; namely, to submit to His righteous rule, enjoy fellowship with Him, behold His glory, and serve Him in worshipful obedience.

Kerygma Narrative

What follows is a narrative of the *kerygma* which reflects the foregoing outline. It includes graphical delineations that can be easily sketched in support of a conversation with a relative, friend, or work associate. Alternatively, you can use this booklet as your guide, in which case I would encourage you to ask your discussion partner to read the Scriptures quoted in the booklet. Also, I recommend that the space available inside and adjacent to the graphical delineations be used for recording insights.

This evangelistic narrative follows the pattern of the so-called Bridge Model, which has been employed for many years as an outline for sharing the Christian gospel.

Dear Friend:

May I have your permission to share what the Bible has to say about our having a relationship with God? The overall flow of what I have to share is outlined in the nearby Figure 3. This should only take about thirty minutes of your time.

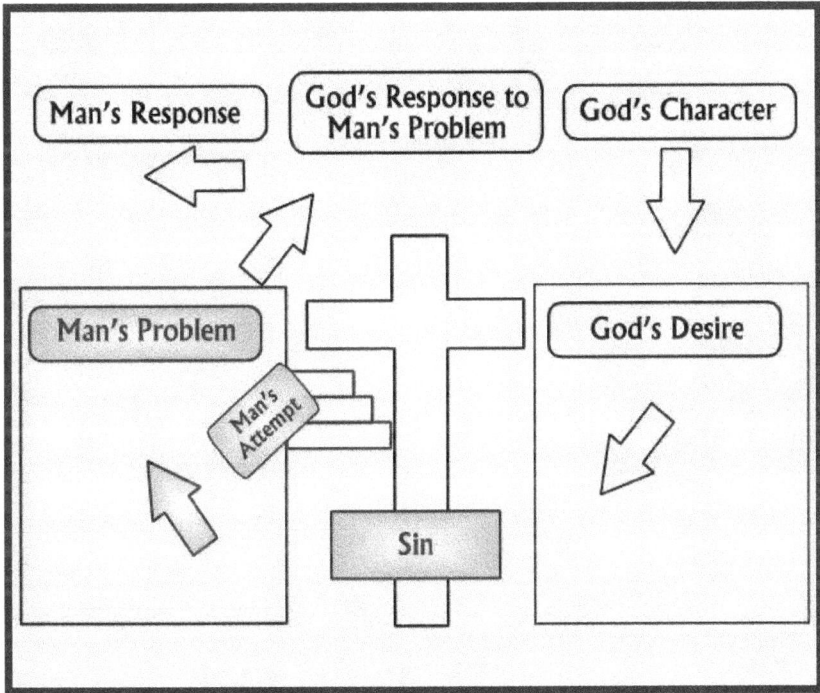

Figure 3. Overall Flow of the Evangelistic Narrative

Figure 3 depicts the gulf that exists between God and man, which is due to the problem of evil, sin, and death. Only Christ's atonement on the Cross can bridge this gulf. The three little bars on the left side of the gulf depict mankind's futile attempts to bridge the gulf, such as through righteous behavior, good deeds, and participation in religious activity. Our conversation will unfold in five distinct stages, beginning with a consideration of God's character.

Stage One: Consideration of God's Character

First, we must consider **God's character** as delineated in Figure 4.

The very first verse in the Bible states,

> **Genesis 1:1.** In the beginning God created the heavens and the earth.

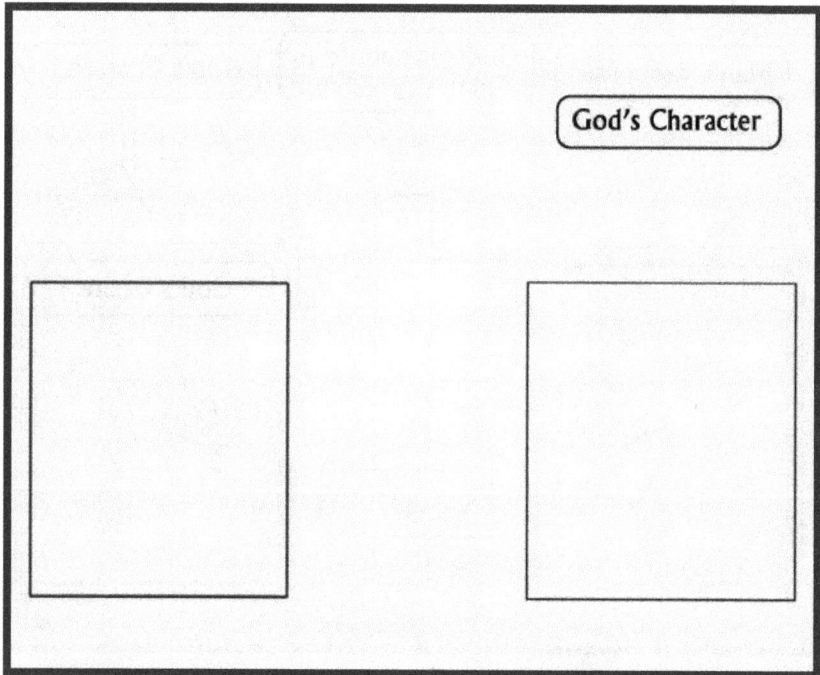

Figure 4. Stage One: Consideration of God's Character

According to the Bible, the Infinite Personal God is Creator of everything. He is before all things, and all His creatures are dependent upon Him and accountable to Him.

While only a few of us have opportunity to actually create or build things from scratch, most of us use things that others have designed and built. We have every right to expect that our computers, cars, appliances, and tools would serve us faithfully according to their designed purpose. In the case of those that do not because of flaws and defects, we attempt to have them repaired, and if they continue to malfunction, we discard and replace them. Our relationship with the things that we use helps us to appreciate God's relationship with us as His creatures. God has every right to expect that we would live and relate to Him and one another according to His purpose and design.

There are three attributes of God's character that are important to our conversation. The first such attribute is His absolute holiness. In the 1st chapter of 1 Peter we read,

> **1 Peter 1:16.** ... Because it is written, "Be holy, for I am holy."

God's holiness includes His transcendence and separateness with respect to His creatures, but also His moral perfection. This is the absolute and inflexible standard that He has set for us in order that we may enjoy fellowship with Him.

The second such attribute is His absolute justice. In the 23rd chapter of Exodus we read,

> **Exodus 23:7b, adapted from the NKJV.** ... For I will not aquit the wicked.

The third such attribute is His divine, self-sacrificial love. In the 4th chapter of 1 John we read,

> **1 John 4:8b.** ... For God is love.

You should be aware of the fact that the word translated **love** in this verse is *agape*, which designates a divine, unconditional, and self-sacrificial love. Only God is capable of this kind of love.

In the 2nd chapter of Genesis, we read how God laid one prohibition upon our first parents, and, in accordance with His absolute holiness and justice, He prescribed the punishment that would result should they disobey His command.

Genesis 2:16-17. And the LORD God commanded the man, saying, "Of every tree of the garden you may freely eat; but of the tree of the knowledge of good and evil you shall not eat, for in the day that you eat of it you shall surely die."

The Bible defines disobedience to the righteous law of God as **sin**. As testified by the passage quoted above, human sin is a capital offense against the holiness and justice of God. The Bible defines three kinds of death that result from human sin: physical death, spiritual death, and eternal death. I will have more to share concerning the problem of evil, sin, and death in the 3rd stage of our conversation.

The absolute justice of God demands that those who pridefully rebel against His righteous rule suffer the punishment of physical, spiritual, and eternal death. However, His absolute love demands that He provide a way to rescue and deliver mankind from our bondage to evil, sin, and death. The manner in which God resolves this dilemma is the content of the Christian gospel that we will unfold as our conversation continues.

Stage Two: Consideration of God's Desire

We next consider **God's desire** for mankind as delineated in Figure 5.

On account of His divine, unconditional, self-sacrificial love, God does not desire that anyone should eternally perish away from His presence, but rather that mankind be rescued from this fate.

This desire is expressed in the 2nd chapter of 1 Timothy where we read,

> **1 Timothy 2:3-4.** ... For this is good and acceptable in the sight of God our Savior, who desires all men to be saved and to come to the knowledge of the truth.

This same desire is expressed in the 3rd chapter of 2 Peter where we read,

> **2 Peter 3:9.** The Lord is not slack concerning His promise, as some count slackness, but is longsuffering toward us, not willing that any should perish but that all should come to repentance.

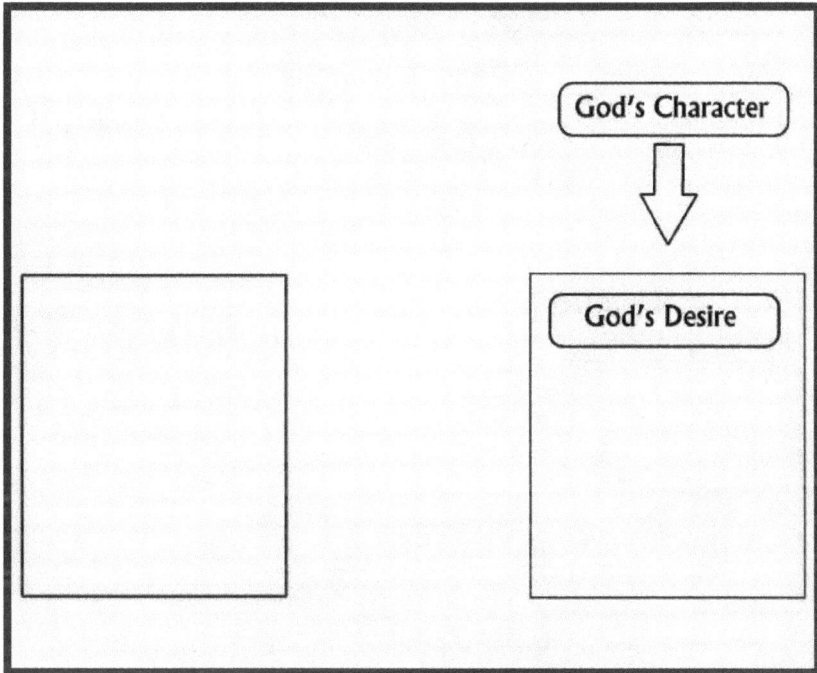

Figure 5. Stage Two: Consideration of God's Desire

God's desire for mankind is expressed in the Old Testament as well, such as in the 18th chapter of Ezekiel, where we read,

> **Ezekiel 18:23.** "Do I have any pleasure at all that the wicked should die?" says the Lord GOD, "and not that he should turn from his ways and live?"

We also find His loving and gracious desire expressed in similar language in Ezekiel 18:32 and Ezekiel 33:11.

Stage Three: Consideration of Man's Problem

As delineated in Figure 6, we next consider **man's problem**.

We have already touched upon the fact that when God created our first parents, Adam and Eve, He laid upon them a single prohibition, which is recorded in Genesis 2:17. God's command regarding the forbidden fruit was not to keep us from enjoying something good, but rather to protect us from experiencing something really bad.

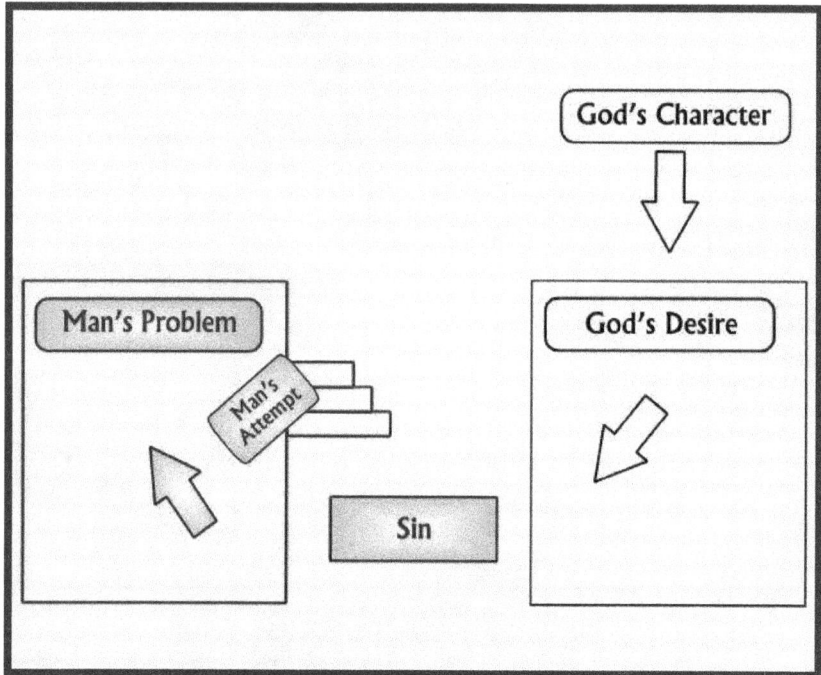

Figure 6. Stage Three: Consideration of Man's Problem

However, according to the 3rd chapter of Genesis, it wasn't long before our first parents fell prey to prideful rebellion against God's righteous rule and partook of the forbidden fruit. This terrible event is what we designate as the **Fall**.

Because of the Fall, prideful rebellion against God's righteous rule has become a governing principle in our hearts, causing us to disobey His commandments, which He put in place for our good. Prideful rebellion against God engenders in each of us all manner of attitudes, thoughts, words, and actions that are contrary to God's righteous and holy character and disobedient to His commandments. These disobedient attitudes, thoughts, words, and actions are what the Bible defines as **sin**.

As taught by the Apostle Paul in the 7th chapter of Romans, our prideful rebellion against the righteous rule of God prompts us to respond to His commandments with an impulse toward disobedience rather than an impulse toward obedience.

The literal meaning of sin is to miss the mark and fall short of the standard of God's righteous and holy commandments. The Bible teaches us that sin is a universal problem. It impacts the life of every man, woman, boy, and girl, as we read in the 3rd chapter of Romans,

> **Romans 3:23.** ... For all have sinned and fall short of the glory of God...

Do you sense that prideful rebellion against the righteous rule of God lurks in your heart, and it causes you to disobey the commandments of God – perhaps only in selfish attitudes and corrupt thoughts? This was certainly my experience before I gave my life to God.

While we may not be as evil and depraved as we could possibly be, with respect to God's absolute standard of moral perfection we all fall short. Our sin is an offense to God. In fact, as we have already noted, our sin is a **capital offense** against God, for which the penalty is death. Therefore, our sins prevent us from submitting to His righteous rule, enjoying fellowship with Him, beholding His glory, and serving Him in worshipful obedience.

As depicted in Figure 6, sin causes a gulf of separation between the human personality and God. In the 59th chapter of Isaiah we read,

> **Isaiah 59:2.** ... But your iniquities have separated you from your God; And your sins have hidden His face from you, so that He will not hear.

Moreover, the ultimate result of our prideful rebellion and sin is eternal separation from God, as we read in 2 Thessalonians 1:7-9.

> **2 Thessalonians 1:7-9.** ... the Lord Jesus is revealed from heaven with His mighty angels, in flaming fire taking vengeance on those who do not know God, and on those who do not obey the gospel of our Lord Jesus Christ. These shall be punished with everlasting destruction from the presence of the Lord and from the glory of His power...

What is the effect of sin on the human personality? In the 6th chapter of Romans we read,

> **Romans 6:23, emphasis added. For the wages of sin is death**, but the gift of God is eternal life in Christ Jesus our Lord.

Thus, our sin bears its hideous fruit in the three kinds of death:

- Physical death, which is separation of the physical body from the immortal spirit.

- Spiritual death, which is separation of the human personality from God during this present life.

- Eternal death, which is eternal separation of the human personality from God in a place of torment.

Because sin is a capital offense against God, **all of us have the sentence of death hanging over our heads**. To illustrate, imagine the situation of a judge who is called upon to administer justice in the case of his son who is accused of murder. While the love of the judge for his son would motivate leniency, justice would demand that the appropriate penalty for the crime be paid if the son is found guilty.

At a more personal level, suppose your neighbor and his family enjoy setting off fireworks in their yard on the 4th of July. However, suppose they set off a rocket that falls on your roof and sets fire to your house. While you may love your neighbor, he needs to take responsibility for the damage done to your house. While God perfectly loves us, our sin remains as a capital offense. His justice must be satisfied in order for Him to lavish upon us the love He desires.

One aspect of the sentence of death is physical death. In the 9th chapter of Hebrews we read,

> **Hebrews 9:27.** And as it is appointed for men to die once, but after this the judgment...

In fact, every time a person dies physically, God's righteous sentence of death is placed in evidence. However, the Bible teaches that physical death does not end our existence, but rather it is the gate through which we pass into an eternal existence, one which is either in God's presence or away from His presence.

> ### *All of us must appear before God's bar of justice.*

Man's Attempt. Men and women around the world, of every nationality, ethnicity, and religious tradition, manifest a consciousness of God, however feeble and misguided it may be. You probably experience this yourself. I certainly did all the years prior to when I gave my life to God. In fact, people universally display a religiosity and a desire to worship someone or something above themselves. Because of this, we engage in various behaviors that are intended to placate God and cause Him to regard us with favor. That is, we attempt to engage in behaviors that are good, charitable toward others, and religious with respect to God. These behaviors are depicted by the three little bars that only partially bridge the gulf between us and God in Figure 6.

Because God created us in His own image and according to His own likeness, there exists in each of us a consciousness of right and wrong. Thus you and I, and many other people that we know, are not as sinful as we might possibly be. In fact, we must affirm the awesome nobility and heroism of which man is capable, especially at times of tragedy.

> ### *However commendable human acts of nobility and heroism may be, they by no means compensate for our sinfulness before God.*

That is why I emphasize prideful rebellion as the governing principle in our hearts that causes us to be disobedient to God's righteous rule in attitudes, thoughts, words, and actions. While you and I may regard ourselves as pretty good people – certainly not as wicked as some people that we know about – we can sense the prideful rebellion in our hearts by the fact that **we are often content to live as if God doesn't exist**. The good deeds and the religious behavior in which we may engage are not done with reference to God and for His glory, but rather they are done with reference to ourselves and for our own glory.

In the 64th chapter of Isaiah we read,

> **Isaiah 64:6.** But we are all like an unclean thing, and all our righteousnesses are like filthy rags; We all fade as a leaf, and our iniquities, like the wind, have taken us away.

Also, in the 3rd chapter of Titus we read,

> **Titus 3:4-6.** But when the kindness and the love of God our Savior toward man appeared, not by works of righteousness which we have done, but according to His mercy He saved us, through the washing of regeneration and renewing of the Holy Spirit, whom He poured out on us abundantly through Jesus Christ our Savior...

In sum, all our attempts to behave righteously and perform good deeds, if done with reference to ourselves and for our own glory, fail to compensate for the prideful rebellion against God that lurks in our hearts.

> *In other words, there is absolutely nothing that we could possibly do that would merit God's favor or cause Him to be pleased with us. Therefore, it is not in our power or ability to effect rescue and deliverance from the problem of prideful rebellion and sin. Rescue and deliverance can only come from God.*

Stage Four: Consideration of God's Response to Man's Problem

As delineated in Figure 7, we next consider **God's response to man's problem**.

To understand and appreciate God's response to man's problem, we must revisit God's character and His desire for us. In my estimation, there is no single passage of Scripture that expresses both of these factors more eloquently than the following passage from the 2nd chapter of Ephesians:

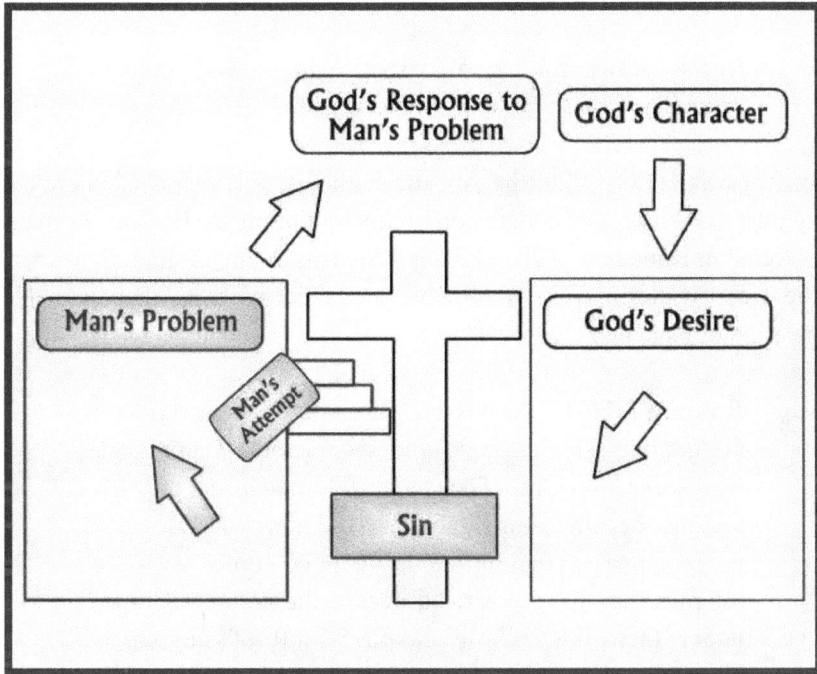

Figure 7. Stage Four: Consideration of God's
Response to Man's Problem

Ephesians 2:1-10, adapted from the NKJV. And you He
made alive, who were dead in trespasses and sins, in which
you once walked according to the course of this world,
according to the prince of the power of the air, the spirit
who now works in the sons of disobedience, among whom
also we all once conducted ourselves in the lusts of our
flesh, fulfilling the desires of the flesh and of the mind, and
were by nature children of wrath, just as the others. But
God, who is rich in mercy, because of His great love with
which He loved us, even when we were dead in trespasses,
made us alive together with Christ (by grace you have been
saved), and raised us up together, and made us sit together
in the heavenly places in Christ Jesus, that in the ages to
come He might show the exceeding riches of His grace as
expressed in His kindness toward us in Christ Jesus. For by
grace you have been saved through faith, and that not of
yourselves; it is the gift of God, not of works, lest anyone
should boast. For we are His workmanship, created in

Christ Jesus for good works, which God prepared beforehand that we should walk in them.

In Romans 1:18 – 3:20, the Apostle Paul sets forth God's indictment against mankind. The conclusion of this section of the Book of Romans is found in Romans 3:9-20, which is actually a litany of quotations from the Hebrew Scriptures. Following are excerpts from that extended passage in Romans:

> **Romans 3:10-19.** As it is written: "There is none righteous, no, not one; There is none who understands; There is none who seeks after God. They have all turned aside; they have together become unprofitable; there is none who does good, no, not one. Their throat is an open tomb; with their tongues they have practiced deceit; the poison of asps is under their lips; whose mouth is full of cursing and bitterness. Their feet are swift to shed blood; destruction and misery are in their ways; and the way of peace they have not known. There is no fear of God before their eyes." Now we know that whatever the law says, it says to those who are under the law, that every mouth may be stopped, and all the world may become guilty before God.

> *The point of Paul's argument is that all men are hopelessly in bondage to evil, sin, and death, and we are powerless to effect rescue and deliverance from this bondage.*

Against this background, in Romans 5:6-11, Paul highlights the unspeakable love of Christ.

> **Romans 5:6-8.** For when we were still without strength, in due time Christ died for the ungodly. For scarcely for a righteous man will one die; yet perhaps for a good man someone would even dare to die. But God demonstrates His own love toward us, in that while we were still sinners, Christ died for us.

Stage Five: Consideration of Man's Response to God

As delineated in Figure 8, we next consider **man's response to God**.

Why would God love the likes of us who, by nature, are hideously offensive to Him? Why would Jesus Christ, the Son of God, die for the likes of us who are in a settled state of prideful rebellion against the righteous rule of God? How should we respond to such extraordinarily self-sacrificial love?

There are two key verbs found in the 1st chapter of Mark's Gospel that define man's appropriate response to God's gracious offer of rescue and deliverance from bondage to evil, sin, and death. Following is the manner in which Jesus introduced the gospel according to Mark's record:

> **Mark 1:15, emphasis added.** "The time is fulfilled, and the kingdom of God is at hand. **Repent**, and **believe** in the gospel."

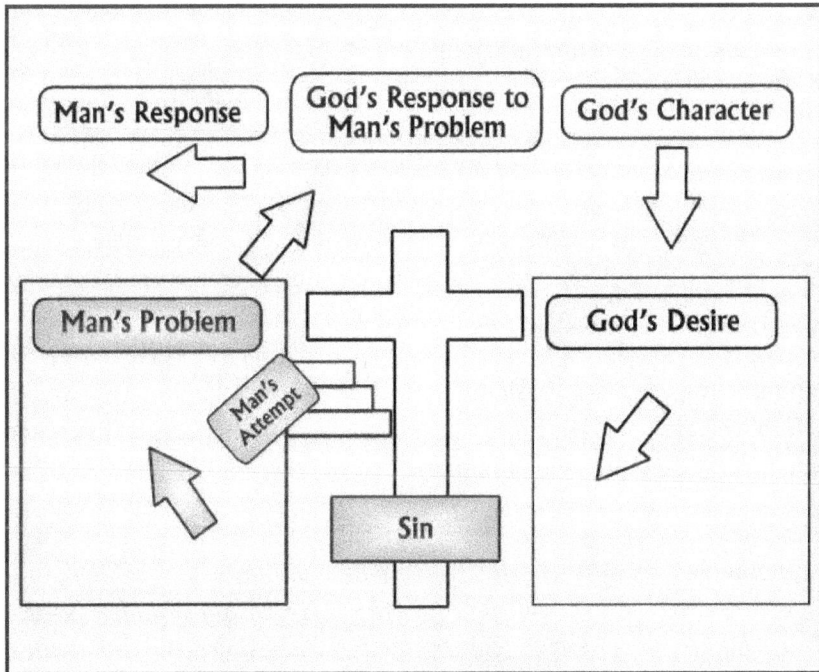

Figure 8. Stage Five: Consideration of Man's Response to God

The two key verbs are **repent** and **believe**. Repent means to change one's mind and the direction of his life. In particular, we must repent of our prideful rebellion against the righteous and holy rule of God and submit to Him as our Creator and King. And we must believe the gospel – that is, embrace it as our only hope of rescue and deliverance from bondage to evil, sin, and death. In particular, we must receive by faith that Jesus' death on our behalf is sufficient to atone for our sin. By means of His death, He paid back to God the Father the infinite debt of apology and satisfaction that each of us owes to Him on account of our sin. From this point forward, we must devote ourselves to following Christ as His obedient disciples.

According to the Bible, God bestows salvation from evil, sin, and death upon all those who embrace Jesus Christ as Savior and Lord in the manner outlined above. Consider the words of Jesus Himself as recorded by the Apostle John in two passages from his Gospel:

> **John 5:24.** "Most assuredly, I say to you, he who hears My word and believes in Him who sent Me has everlasting life, and shall not come into judgment, but has passed from death into life."

> **John 1:12-13.** But as many as received Him, to them He gave the right to become children of God, to those who believe in His name: who were born, not of blood, nor of the will of the flesh, nor of the will of man, but of God.

Not only is God the Father ready, willing, and able to forgive us, but He joyfully embraces us as adopted children and members of His family. Moreover, He sends His Spirit into our hearts to motivate, strengthen, and establish us in a lifestyle of holiness.

> *By means of His Spirit, He enables us to begin to live in accordance with the purpose for which He designed and created us; that is, to submit to His righteous rule, enjoy fellowship with Him, behold His glory, and serve Him in worshipful obedience.*

Conclusion: Your Response to the Gospel

There you have the Christian gospel. The question that you must answer for yourself is this: "Where am I located in the diagram?" Many people respond by putting themselves in the middle, as shown in Figure 9.

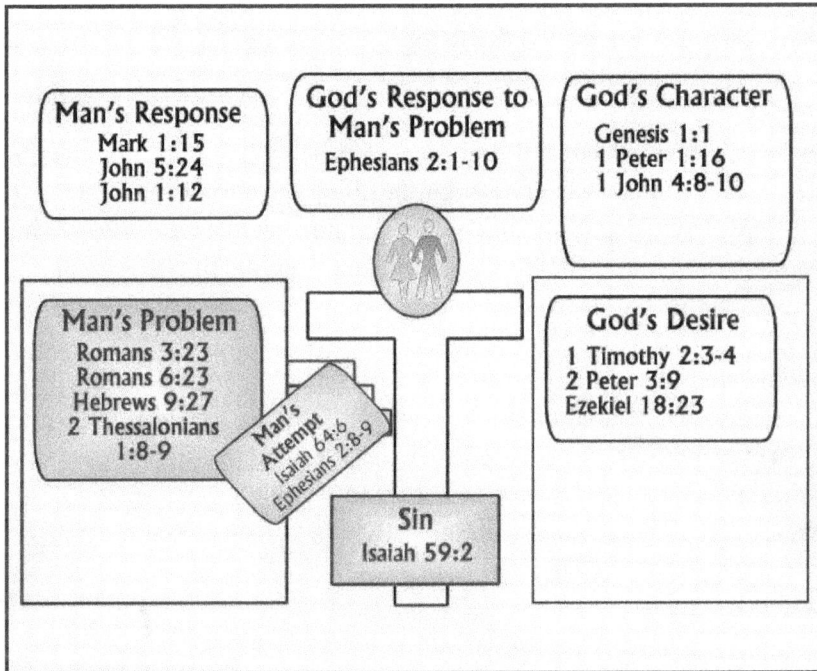

Figure 9. Conclusion: Your Response to the Gospel

This seems like a safe answer, but actually it is unworkable, like being half born or half married. The Bible clearly states that each and every one of us is either on one side of the diagram or the other – either a member of God's family or not. If you sense God drawing you to Himself through what we have shared, then it would be good for you to respond to Him as outlined below:

- Repent and turn away from your prideful rebellion against the righteous and holy rule of God.

- Believe the gospel and embrace it heartily as your only hope of rescue and deliverance from bondage to evil, sin, and death.

- Trust in and appropriate Jesus' death on your behalf whereby God is enabled to forgive you completely, declare you to be righteous in His sight, give you eternal life, and embrace you as an adopted child and a member of His family.

- Wholeheartedly resolve to follow Jesus from this point forward as His obedient disciple.

- Open your heart to the ministry of the Holy Spirit of God, whereby you will be enabled to begin fulfilling the purpose for which you were created: to submit to God's righteous rule, enjoy fellowship with Him, behold His glory, and serve Him in worshipful obedience.

I know that this is a monumental and life-changing decision which you presently face. Based on the promises of Scripture as confirmed by my own experience, I can assure you that this is a good decision, and one that you'll never regret. I would love to help you with this decision if you would care to correspond with me.

Yours in Christ,

Peter Briggs

Peter Briggs, Ph.D.
Founder & President of Daystar Institute
of Biblical Theology & Leadership Development
Email: DaystarInstituteNM@gmail.com

Walking in the Way of Christ & the Apostles

Study Guide Series (SGs)

Part 1 – Foundational Concepts. These concepts are foundational to equip the Christ-follower to have and to be governed by the mind of Christ.

1. The Way of God
2. The Storyline of the Bible
3. Biblical Reality
4. Discovering the Meaning of Scripture
5. Torah: The Fountainhead of Wisdom
6. The Two-Part Christian Gospel

Part 2 – The Gospel of the Kingdom of God. Here we explore the ways in which the Christian gospel confronts the prideful rebellion of the human heart and exalts Christ as King over all.

7. Authority of the King
8. Called by the King
9. Meaning of Discipleship
10. Disciplines of the Kingdom
11. Household of the King
12. Second Coming of the King

Part 3 – The Gospel of God. This final set explores how the Christian gospel affords a complete solution to human depravity and the threefold problem of evil, sin, and death.

13. Introduction to the Gospel of God
14. Reason for the Gospel of God
15. Content of the Gospel of God
16. Perversions of the Gospel of God
17. Application of the Gospel of God

Theological Readers (TRs)

TR1 – Part 1: Foundational Concepts
TR2 – Part 2: The Gospel of the Kingdom of God
TR3 – Part 3: The Gospel of God
TR4 – Resources and Appendices

Connect with us at www.DaystarInstituteNM.us, or
Contact us via email at WalkingintheWayUSA@gmail.com

Walking in the Way of
Christ & the Apostles

www.ingramcontent.com/pod-product-compliance
Lightning Source LLC
Chambersburg PA
CBHW071807020426
42331CB00008B/2425